Line Drawing

Line Drawing
Ross Wilson

Smokestack Books
1 Lake Terrace, Grewelthorpe, Ripon HG4 3BU
e-mail: info@smokestack-books.co.uk
www.smokestack-books.co.uk

Text copyright 2018,
Ross Wilson,
all rights reserved.

ISBN 9781999674205

Smokestack Books
is represented
by Inpress Ltd

for Amanda

I was here, where you are,
looking down on this paper

to discover what we share,
to uncover where we part,

to see the lines between,
to seek the lines that join.

Contents

Thinking	9
Line Drawing	10
You Don't Hit a Man When He's Down	12
What's in Our Hands	13
Ex-Factory Toun	14
Outside a Castle	16
Routes	17
Jist a Hoosewife	18
The ABC	19
Across the Tracks	21
Sweet Promise	23
The Auld Patterns	24
Ex-Mining Village, Xmas Day	26
Antonine Wall, Croy Hill	27
Likes	28
Daylight Robbery	29
Thieves	30
The Law	31
Worth	32
The Heavy Bag	33
Esplanade	35
After Work	36
Anithir Season	37
The Way John Went Out	39
Context	41
Sticks 'n' Stones	43
A Pint in Plato's Cave	44
Domestic Dispute	45
Nursing Games	46
The Pod	47
Roots	48
The In-gaun Ee	49
Guddling	50
Sparks	51
Bertie's Drum	52

The Sweet Science	53
Bedside Cabinet	54
The ABC 2	55
A Handshake in Thought	56
Chuvalo	57
Adam's Terrace	58
Flight	61
Notes	63
Acknowledgements	65

Thinking

Who knows what started it?
Probably not the man who hit
his brother, or the brother who hit
the floor. Probably not the girl,
her rouged lips a wound spurting,
ih's yir brithir!
ih's yir brithir!
I lost interest, wondering
if this spot by Dunfermline Abbey,
this club, *Life*, was where
Henryson wrote his fables,
and if thinking is what separates us
from animals.

Who knows what Cain was thinking,
cuffed in a van. Or Abel, buried
with the cause of all the trouble
under a rubble of chairs and glass.
Or the war-painted banshee
wailing like the Black Douglas
when he charged into blackness
seven hundred years ago, the heart
of the Bruce in his fist like a bomb
to throw in some Holy War
in the name of God or
some such thing our
thinking inspires us to fight over.

Line Drawing

Lines were scored in the dirt in early boxing matches when a knockdown, not a bell, concluded a round; if a pugilist couldn't 'toe the line' or come 'up to scratch,' he was ruled Out of Time.

To deter members of opposing parties from attacking one another in the House of Commons two red lines were marked, two swordlengths apart, on the floor. MPs were and are expected to stand behind these lines when a speech is in progress.

Emerging from Southwark Station,
looking for Tate Modern,
I imagined this area back when
bear-baiting and cock-fighting were common,
and actors strutted their hour at the Globe.
Stumbling on the Ring Boxing Club,
I thought, how appropriate
a space to exhibit the noble art
should be so near the Tate.
Then, a second thought
that was more of a picture:
Two-Ton Tony Galento, a boxer
from the thirties who trained on beer
and refused to shower weeks before
a fight; who, according to Max Baer,
stank 'like rotten tuna and old liquor
sweated out;' who, when asked
what he thought of Shakespeare,
said, *'I'll moider da bum!'*
A hairy bear of a man, Two-Ton Tone
applied gouging, biting, butting, low blows
and kidney punching to what some
call the sweet science, others, the noble art.
In black and white footage of him
he brightens the screen like a cartoon.
The owner of a New Jersey saloon.

I saw him clearly in London
four hundred years ago, betting on
a chained bear versus dogs,
and toeing the line
men have always drawn in the grime.

You Don't Hit a Man When He's Down

To write about boxing is to be forced to contemplate not only boxing, but the perimeters of civilization – what it is, or should be, to be 'human.'
Joyce Carol Oates, *On Boxing*

I remember watching Frazier v Bugner.
Bugner was out on his feet,
Frazier about to him him again
before the referee could intervene.

Set to deliver a final punch,
this champion of violence stopped,
stepped back and let his victim
sag to the canvas in a delayed reaction.

What sportsmanship! What sportsmanship!
The commentator announced.
Those words and images returned to me
as I watched a man go down hard in a cage

while another ran at the prone body
to hit it again and again until,
finally, the referee pulled him back
like the auld saying:

You don't hit a man when he's down
used to restrain us, or most of us,
like a proverb few remember
as other ideas pollute the air,

whispering into the ear:
Survival of the fittest.
Strong eat the weak.
No such thing as society.

What's in Our Hands

How could a man hit a man with a hammer?
We know the reason – drug-money.
But how could he grab and raise and swing
such a thing as a hammer, and bring
it down upon the head of another?

I once hit a man so hard his nose burst
over his trainers. Later, he laughed
at it still bleeding after a shower;
we'd been sparring, practising for
the real thing with big sixteen oz gloves.

A skinny teenager did that
with one left hook – my weak arm.
The hand I write with is stronger. It asks:
how could a man hit a man with a hammer?
And holds the answer in itself.

Ex-Factory Toun

Boab attended a Cambridge lecture
on the moral philosopher and economist,
Adam Smith.

Tired after a shift selling stuff,
the *tsk* of his lager can didn't bring one
tut to a student lip:

the lecture, a recording on Youtube,
was at least five years old
and thousands of miles away

from his home town, Kirkcaldy.
Kirk caddy, the lecturer called it,
but what did he ken?

What ye watchin' that fir?
Boab's wife demanded to know,
that's no fir the likes ih us.

He had to pause and scroll back
to what her voice made him miss;
someone had asked a question:

did Adam Smith
define wealth as money?
No, well-being.

A few days ago, Boab ate a pie
by the High Street bakers, observing
a plaque consumers ignore,

explaining how Adam Smith lived here,
and how this was where
he wrote *The Wealth of Nations*.

Boab had thought a visitor
could be forgiven for thinking
Kirkcaldy was called Toilet.

TO LET signs jutted over
shut shops all around him.
Under one,

the bollard of a beggar
was avoided by a man
on his way to the Jobcentre,

a Jobseeker's Allowance booklet
stuffed into his back pocket
like an empty wallet;

the image of it clear as old photos
Boab had seen of the town's
linoleum and linen factories,

now shut down, or in ruin.
Boab scratched his belly, feeling
something had to be in gestation.

For things had to change soon,
he thought, reaching
for another cold can.

Outside a Castle

We argued outside a castle.
He wouldn't go in.
His seat belt held him back
like a cord needing cut –
he'd not forgotten what
he'd been born into: *wi'd nuthin.'*

Aye, then, I protested, pointing
to what men had built with their own
hands and imaginations.
He saw calloused fingers sifting hours
into monuments for their betters.
I saw no point being bitter.

He sat it out,
a protester in his eightieth-year rebellion,
while my palm turned over
hard-earned minimum wages
for a guided tour of privileges
far removed from his ruined raws.

Routes

in memory of Aund Paterson, 1925-2010

I remember ticking *no religion*
in my first job-application form.
'Yir a Protestant,' he told me.
'No, Ah'm no,' I told him.

At his funeral a Catholic neighbour
said, year after year,
he signed Christmas cards *comrade*.
Things aren't always as they appear.

Escape routes connected the pits
in case of disaster.
That's another thing he told me.
Years later I see disused routes

under the fields and streets
between men, and imagine
lifelines buried in fists
blooming into palms.

Jist a Hoosewife

in memory of Ena Paterson, 1924-2015

That's what they called her –
jist a hoosewife.
I thought about that
as we crossed the Forth.

To the right of us
the rail bridge –
a work of art
exhibited in space.

To the left,
the new road bridge
emerging from water.
I thought of all the foundations

holding roads and rails up
and together.
And I thought of her,
unacknowledged worker,

essential as any commuter
on a road suspended in air.
Jist a pillar,
they might have said you were.

Jist a pillar that holds us up
and keeps us going,
though hidden under water
as if you weren't there.

The ABC (Amateur Boxing Club)

Wee Barry was first – his first bout.
Three rounds with a twelve-year-old double.
    Mirror images until
the glass shattered like a dream
    and reality battered his wee face red.
        Barry cried in the changing room:
ma nose hurts like hell!
    Only a point in it, Alec said,
        ye done well.

Then there was Sean.
    Features ghosted with nerves,
        Sean flushed vomit and
seconds out, minutes later, was hit
    out of time. A wee one asked: *did it hurt?*
        No! The pain
was several inches south of the blow.
    Sean didn't bleed:
        blood bloomed his cheeks.

Lanky Colin jabbed and crossed, dangling
    danger on the end of two rods,
        a smug grin as each jab went in and in.
In the closing seconds a hook sank into
    his burger-Coke-lined guts. Winded,
        he grappled a pummelling desperado, until
the bell, sweet as his girl the night before.
    Colin won by a score:
        nineteen hits to four.

Next, John. A Scottish champion six years
    before nightlife blackened his eyes
        darker than any glove ever did.
Body hardened by Saughton's gym,
    arms colourful as an exotic bird's wings,
        rage carried him into the ring, through two
wild rounds into a third. Drained as a
    pint glass, a white towel fluttered
        to save him from himself.

Dean! Dean always broke the circle training –
    facing a mirror as the rest faced one another.
        i-pod in ear, deaf to instruction,
Dean danced, vaulting the ropes.
    But a boot snagged and tumbled him
        and laughter bellowed around the ring.
It was hell after that. Pride punctured,
    body blows deflated the rest.
        His record fell: four wins, now a loss.

Last: eighteen, unbeaten, Andy sat
    staring at boots that run miles
        every night they don't skip rope in a gym.
No one will fight him: *too much power, skill.*
    There are whispers of other countries;
        talk of a blue vest.
I've no passport,
    he told Alec.
        Your passport's talent 'n' will.

Weekends Alec drives a transit van full
    of bleeding noses, bruised ribs, battered egos.
        Sixty years old and so alive his breath
is a winter plume against a darkened windscreen.
    Half-way cross-country tonight.
        Tomorrow: a roof with hammer and slate.
Alec smiles into a mirror full of boys
    sleepy with dreams or dreaming awake:
        the future is full of girls and fighting.

Across the Tracks

Across the border they'd be chavs.
Here, they're neds, and almost proud,
as if to be a ned was to have a trade;
their tracksuits overalls,
Buckfast bottles tools.

They drink by a stone in a park
near a railway station in the dark
unable to see what the stone's
supposed to be. A lighter reveals
words about a civil war in Spain.

Across the rails a memorial garden
is maintained for lives laid down
in the Great War for Civilisation
and all the wars that came
after civilisation was won.

Wiy's this stane here, no there?
What made this war diffrint?
Ma pal's pal wis killt in Afghanistan –
what stane will his name be oan?
Just then, headlights of a police van

across the road, hit them
like an interrogation light, bright
with questions of its own.
A voice called like a cue to act out
the role they'd been given

or the life they'd chosen,
depending on what side of the line
we choose to see them from.
Near a public library and museum,
art gallery and memorial garden,

across the tracks, on the steps
of the Adam Smith Theatre, a man
and woman exit *Macbeth*
as three boy-men run by a train
and enter a scene they've no part in.

Sweet Promise

The soldiers appear happy
on the poster in the bus shelter
I glance at on my way home.
A phrase 'This is belonging,'
drifts like a plume of smoke from a gun
above the lads' jolly camaraderie.

I remember something a friend once told me –
a woman, burdened by shopping,
was walking towards him
and the Asda he was leaving.
She'd been to a foodbank,
she explained as he offered a hand.

Her man had belonged
to a unit operating in Iraq.
His benefits had been cut.

I think of that as I pass the shelter.
It sits across the road from a high school
like a trap baited with a slogan
luring the young, as if
this box to keep out the rain
is a haven, whispering
the sweet promise of belonging.

The Auld Patterns

How old would I have been?
More accurate to ask, how young?
Twenty-one or so, lining up to clock in
to a factory full of women
and half-a-dozen men, pleating.
Reading on my break how K
could never get into the castle
was like reading some reversal
to my own situation in Castleblair:
Despair, I called it. I was there
when 9/11 happened,
pushing a trolley full of patterns,
hot from an autoclave;
I overheard talk of a plane flying
into a building, thought it was some
inane far-fetched film. Now,
Castle Despair is in ruin.
Then they were talking
of transferring the labour to Turkey.
We didn't care, we were
only ever temporary, always ready
to move on. Twelve-hour shifts,
minimum wage, standing by huge tables,
unrolling, clipping, fixing material
quickly but delicately, then
pulling the cover over, rolling
tight scrolls we'd tie with rags
and discard like giant cigars,
before starting over and over and over . . .
Sometimes we'd look up, over
a factory floor buzzing with women.
It was as though they were making
themselves on the production lines where
they'd stitch and sew and perspire
and peer up and down and stare

at the pleaters fingering material.
In our early twenties still, minutes
from a bar, hours from the feel
of soft fabric hugging her,
or her, or her, or whoever . . .
My hands would bleed and blister:
the head pleater had never
seen such sensitive skin
in twenty years of pleating.
Even my lips cracked in the heat:
I'd taste blood talking.
I'd taste blood laughing.
I'd feel blood pleating.
I only got the job because a man
punched another man in the face
and had to be replaced:
we can't condone such behaviour.
A year later, boys I went to school with wore
a new uniform: guns in place of pens, war
replacing lessons.
How old would we have been?
Old enough for anything,
young enough for thinking
to take second place to feeling.
We felt the material we'd been given:
we fixed it into the auld patterns.

Ex-Mining Village, Xmas Day

The flat at the end of the street
looks like an advent calendar,
though I doubt anything sweet
would be found on the other
side of its boarded windows.

On a day to give gifts, someone
has bricked and egged a neighbour.
Yolk slimes the pebbledash
like glue holding the words
JUNKIE SCUM together.

Antonine Wall, Croy Hill

To get here we had to pass stained mattresses,
used condoms, palettes, spare tyres,
the blackened remains of fires
where teenagers burned rubbish
locals had strewn about.

To get here we had to skirt
the former mining village, Croy.
Fenced off from this historic site
by an ugly spiked railing that could have been
legions of spears in line.

I saw Roman soldiers here, Caledonians there,
recalled the Kelty Caveman tag I'd been
labeled with at school, the mining villages
let go, Glasgow, so close by,
the Effect it's known by.

To get here, 1,860 years had to fly
from this man-made ditch
to a twenty-first century division –
a health gap that doesn't cut the land
but scars the nation.

Likes

Facebook 'selfies for cancer' inspired her
to empty a cupboard in her Mum's kitchen,
photo the empty shelves, and post:
SHELFIES FOR FOOD BANKS
with a link to send donations.

No one 'liked' it. Some were angry.
Cancer victims don't choose cancer.
Who did *she* know who used food banks?
Why encourage charity for scroungers?
They've enough money for fags and drugs.

Her mum thought it a great lesson:
never discuss politics or religion
on Facebook or, well, anywhere *ever*.
Oh, remember the selfie you posted?
Remember all the 'likes' it generated?

No one wants to think about ugly things,
people want to see nice pretty things
like you, her mum explained, re-stocking
the shelves with tin after tin after tin,
then forcing the door shut, to keep them in.

Daylight Robbery

'Junkie bastard broke in,
broad daylight. Can ye imagine?
Tried tae wrench the door wi a crowbar,
then took a brick tae the windae.'
I imagined a face reflected in glass,
a brick smashing features like stone
shattering calm water in a loch,
affecting everyone within
the rippling of its concentric span.
The glass house would have been
much easier to break in had the robber seen
any value between its panes.
As my neighbour went on,
I remembered something a pal once said,
'Ken where the sayin
daylight robbery comes fae?
Windae tax. Imagine piyin fir sunshine!
No sun, where's the light a bairn's brain will grow?
But why would my neighbour
contemplate talk of nature and nurture?
He was the victim here.
'It makes ye wonder,' I began,
'what drives a man . . . '
'*They* make thir ayn decisions.
Wiv aw choices: some work so
they can afford keys tae enter rooms
thiv bought; ithirs think bricks acceptable
tae open doors thiv closed oan thirsel.'
It dawned on me then I didn't even know his name.
How long had we lived in the same building?
'Hope they get him,'
I said, opening my door and reaching down
for a letter I was soon to discover
concerned my spare bedroom.

Thieves

He attacked his pal with a shovel
as if it were a sword.
It cracked a palette-shield
doubling as a weapon, blocking,
ramming the shovel-wielding man
whose foreign tongue spat venom
as the shovel swung again.
    It was 2 a.m.
They were fighting about the overtime
one had stolen from the other.
They'd been bussed in from Glasgow:
    Kosovans.

Weeks later, on another factory floor,
I heard news of that other place
employing illegal immigrants.
    Cunts ir stealin oor joabs,
a man along the line said.
Months later, we were laid off,
our work sent abroad,
our feet sent to the Jobcentre.
I found work in a hotel
near the fault lines where
high and low lands clash.
The only Scot among East Europeans,
living under conference rooms
where men in suits clicked pens.

The Law

Mother laid down the law –
don't be selfish, don't be greedy,
share all your toys.

Decades later, she cast
a new light on the big boys
exposing cracks in the clear line
she'd always drawn
between right and wrong.

A politician, criticising the
'something for nothing culture'
refused to answer a question:
'What's your opinion
of corporate tax havens?'

Mother answered for him –
'Well, it's not against the law,
is it son?'

Worth

A finger contacts a pupil.
A twenty-five year-old face,
ten years ahead of itself, blinks
into focus.

A twisted sneer turns
from a mirror.
A hand grabs flab
bulging off a belly.

Irn Bru washes breakfast down –
crisps, diet pills.
A chapped lip hooks a fag –
pink finger-nails fill

a tracksuit with tattooed limbs.
A chakit face coughs a curse
at *that place* where
pettiness chokes the air

like the nooses her pierced lip
puffs aff a crabbit sneer.
A bitter breath sighs
between yellow teeth.

And because some things
are hard to face,
or admit, her eyes glisten
under contacts circled by

mascara-snares blinking shut
on a mind full of its own shit,
on a world viewed through
lashes bared like teeth,

on a life existed, not lived,
minimum wages by the hour.

The Heavy Bag

He forced hands into gloves
tense as cats stuffed into bags,
thumbs thrust tight into corners
like men cut off from others,
anger forging flesh and bone
into weapons to employ, lightly
at first, each fist swatting dust
the summer breeze swirls.
He's already broken sweat
running home so fast as if,
in gaining pace, he could run
away from what he had to do
to earn a living, heart
battering the cage it's in
hard, fast, expanding
red as the gloves now hitting
the heavy bag: jab, hook, cross, jab.
The bag twists and turns into a boss,
colleague, banker, politician . . .
a shape-shifting shadow,
a doppelgänger waiting
to counter his least error.
His limbs form armour
from imaginary blows. He throws
one-twos like dance partners:
left leads – right follows through,
and his body explodes into
this bag designed to endure.
It jolts on a rope hooked to a rafter.
Its bulk sways like a suicide
in the breeze that catches her
scent before he sees
or feels a shoulder take the weight.
He steps back, then in, to meet
lips with his own, and takes her

into arms now open and warm.
Gloves off, fists bud fingers,
and palms feel the throb
behind the rib, and absorb
the beating bag.

Esplanade

Eyes stinging from a nightshift,
he sees vague shapes shift
in the early morning haar,
hears foghorns like buzzers,
the distant hum of cars,
the rattling breath of a man.
His sweat mingles with fumes
on the salt sea air.

A stench lingers from earlier.
Eyes shut:
hands fold a sheet
over a man's face.

It's almost dawn.
The esplanade is in need
of regeneration;
waves smash it like years
crash against flesh and bone.

Soon, spring will return.
Sooner still, the sun will burn
into his black-out curtains
as his arms gather her
warm breathing to him,
his chest beating into her spine.

After Work

With tired limbs stretching
and a yawn snatching words
like a bird swallowing flies,
and the duvet warm over skin,
and the soft arm draping
a meal-swollen belly
like a belt buckling him
into dream, he forgot
about the alarm: silent
as a sniper under cover
of mug and book –
the cold dark set in its sights.

Anithir Season

in memory of Alec 'Spangles' Hunter, 1936-1995

When they found Marciano's body
strapped in the crashed plane seat,
someone said start counting, he'll get up.
He always did, when he was down.

I remembered that story the day
Spangles went down.

A sweet tooth behind a bark:
thir'll be no fuckin' swearin in this gym!
A face marked by 626 fights.
At fifty-nine, he went down refereeing a bout
with no one to replace him to take up a count
that went by so fast we had our doubts
it was over.

That's anithir season yeh'v wastit!
He'd say when I'd return to the gym
years after my last fight,
and with more appetite
for the atmosphere than the blows
that carved and cut and shaped him
like a pumpkin fired within.

Anithir season wastit
as though he thought I'd be back.
As though to say: he's just resting.
I was young after all.

Now, I hit harder with the weight
time packs into a punch, and slower,
with energy that saps like the sweat
I watch drip away, wondering
what Spangles would say
about this new club full of women
and bairns and music – attitudes
shaped by the seasons he's been gone.

His voice plays on – an old record
scratched and scored as his face,
and turning in my memory:
This isnae a fuckin' youth club!
As if to say: this isn't a game.
You don't *play* boxing.

Months after the old club
was knocked down and out of existence
the headline read:
Final Round for Boxing Legend.

That was 1995.
This is another century, another gym
with the same fighting spirit alive
in twelve-year-olds I watch spar
and prepare fir anithir season.

The Way John Went Out

in memory of John Gray

I had you in my corner a few years,
talking me into, and through pain.

Weekends, you'd take me into
Edinburgh and Glasgow to train;
mid-week, we worked out in Rosyth.
Days in-between, I ran alone.

We were about the same height then:
Five-three, flyweights. I, fourteen, all bone,
you, a trim forty, fitter than anyone
in the gym, until I caught up, like time

caught us, six years later.
A six-foot welterweight that day
we met, books tucked under what had been
a left hook, specs on a never-broken nose.

I was awoken that day
like a brawler too clumsy to duck
the surprise counter of your news.
The best punches come from nowhere.

This one hit before we could begin.
A doctor stepped between us, waving it all off;
a timekeeper beat the slow count out of days
before a bell could ring.

And it was a daze to stumble into,
like those nights when I'd run alone
in the dark of a wood, no stool to rest on,
and no voice in the corner where I once stood

tired and bloodied with your hand
flying my hand like the kite
we were both high as, walking
down the steps of Meadowbank

Stadium, 1993. *You came in with nothing,*
you said to me, *you went out a champion.*

Context

for Keith Mitchell

I know Keith is in because the drunks
congregating by the wine shop
beneath his flat are pointing and shouting at
the wide-open window and speaker
positioned on the sill blasting Wagner
down upon them like boiling oil
pouring from a castle turret into their ears –
the artist under siege in his ivory tower!

I let myself in and manoeuvre around
canvases rolled, framed, stacked in a hall
like a production line managed by a Bohemian,
each painting uniquely its own.
The sun spotlights an easel set up
in the living room where Keith
is busy painting *Columbo
and the Crucifixion.*

It's upside down, I tell him,
as if that's news to him.
It's easier to paint that way, he tells me.
YIR MUSIC'S SHITE! They tell us, so,
Keith cranks the volume and shows me
a bust he sculpted out of chocolate.
I call it, Chocolate David Icke, he says,
reaching for a bottle of Johnny Walker.

In cafes and bars I've been taken as his carer
when his Dandy garb and arty gub
rubs locals the wrong way and rips
eyelids from faces that sway
back from his presence like a punch.
When asked where he's from: *Kelty,*
people tell him:
ir ye fuck!

But in his studio-flat or gallery
when they can see the evidence
of what he does, of who he is,
mouths shut, eyes open,
imaginations bloom.
YouTubing John Coltrane,
Keith pours a dram, explains:
I make sense in this context.

Sticks 'n' Stones

When Thomas Aikenhead exited a bar
rubbing his hands together
like a caveman trying to light a fire,
he wasn't to know the friction he caused
would produce a spark that would leap
down centuries and blaze so hard
we still feel the heat 300 years after
the Kirk hanged him for blasphemy.

I thought of him today while reading
about a gay teenager thrown from a building,
an adulteress stoned to death,
and the outraged thoughts of friends,
their centrally-heated hands
fluttering, free as birds, to use
whatever words they choose
to silence language they find offensive.

A Pint in Plato's Cave

Sometimes the stories we tell
cast shadows on the wall.
On the big screen, Mel
fought for freedom while
the flesh-and-blood, warts-'n'-all
Wallace flayed de Cressingham
to make a scabbard for his sword
out of the treasurer's skin.

I remember arguing with a man
who had a badge of Lenin
on his bunnet. We were in a place known
as Little Moscow.
He had a pish stain on his jeans.
The colour of his lager
made me imagine his brain
was a catheter his tongue would drain.

I prefer to get drunk on beer
than ideas filtering down through a bar.
What's propaganda but hot air?
There's no left or right to shite –
stink diffuses far and wide,
and where fuses are short
explosions are inevitable;
even Jesus kicked over a table.

It takes a foot on the ground
to give abstractions a kicking.
It takes a boot rising up
to make cracks in the wall
for light to spill in.
Plaster and paint them as you will,
sometimes the stories we tell
cast shadows over us all.

Domestic Dispute

'Though they styled themselves members of the radical left, they could be outrageously arrogant toward the people who had to clean up after them.'
Jonathan Rose, *The Intellectual Life of the British Working Classes*

The domestic sat in one room,
the social justice activists in another.
She could hear their voices
though nothing they said was clear.

The wall that came between them
was laid on a foundation of hot air;
they'd built it from the clouds down
rather than the ground up, so when

the likes of Agnes called a bin liner
a 'black bag' they could send her
to a room for vulgar racists to wait in,
before she had to clean up after them.

Nursing Games

The nurses took position
for the hundred-metre hurdle,
each focusing on the patient
bedded at the end of their lane.

The call bell was the signal
that sent them running,
leaping cold metal filing cabinets,
racing towards the buzzing lights.

The first to reach her patient
was the loser. The winner
had stopped to shuffle papers,
tick sheets, file forms.

But I won, the loser protested.
No, you did not, she was told,
for if it wasn't written,
it wasn't done.

The Pod

The pod on the wall
of his room in the hospital
contained his cigarettes.
Visitors thought he had Tourette's,

the way he'd roar and curse
'that wee lassie,' the nurse
who had the key to his fags.
He needed a smoke, not jags.

He was sixty now and Korsakoff's
had been diagnosed. Handcuffs
was the word he heard them say.
They didn't want him getting away

like the youth long since escaped
into a past now largely draped
in a dark curtain, though gaps
let some light in to the trap,

illuminating snatches of time
like when he and his pals were nine,
burying treasure in a garden,
drawing maps to find it later on.

He liked to play at pirates
before he played with cigarettes,
or was played with by alcohol
and reduced to smashing a pod on a wall

with a zimmer or walking stick.
They made him fucking sick.
Was all this some bad joke?
All he needed was a smoke.

Roots

Roots are nourishing.
Roots haud ye back.

He was flourishing when
his boots stopped in their tracks.

Where ye hink yir gaun?
A voice demanded in a bark,

tongues snaring his shins
like heavy chains or straps.

Or anchors dragging him down
to earth like it was a trap

and not something to grow in
or drink from like a tap.

Roots are nourishing.
Roots haud ye back.

The In-gaun Ee

The walls were cold as the dungeon
I pretended the cellar was, as a bairn.
Webs netted my hair when I stepped in,
stooping to scrape a shovel into the dark pile
and haul a bucket full of coal into the light
like the black box from the wreckage
of an age locked in the head.

What I felt, smelt, heard in that cellar
was fitted in me with the gas fire,
then dipped into like a hoard years later:
the in-gaun ee of a mine
I enter again and again.

Guddling

'No man ever steps in the same river twice, for it's not the same river and he's not the same man.'
Heraclitus

Two decades ago I dipped my hands
into a burn, hooking fingers
under boulders, feeling for skin
beneath skull-like stone.

One moment nothing, then
something darts from dirt water
under lashed lids where
survivors hide, until stirred...

Twenty seconds ago, a few hours
twenty years before tore through me –
I was a bairn again, guddling
a reflection moving in a burn.

Sparks

for Andy Paterson

Sparks spit in the brain
like the cinder my cousin
witnessed as a bairn
loup from the fire upon
the rug and burn
before an auld miner spat on
his fingers, turning fleshy-bone
into pincers to pinch and fling
that ember back into the flame.

He must have been
wide-eyed as my nieces,
decades later, hypnotised by
their first-ever coal fire:
colourful as a spaceship
landed from another planet,
the crackling smoking amazing
heat of it, licking black lumps
of ice cream, melting into ash.

Bertie's Drum

in memory of Bertie Hutchison

Bertie beamed as he drummed
the big bass drum auld Aund
beat upon when he was a bairn.

Memory fired by a dram,
he imagined that drum before him,
re-creating his uncle's moves –

hands burling apart
meeting again by the magnet
of his heart.

The Sweet Science

Words lost the commentators
in thought fogs they thought were clear
but were not – anything but.
In this confused mist of things in conflict
lines are scored between eyes
like the lines old pugilists had to toe.
Now two girls approach that old scratch,
and an uncomfortable itch
has two former boxers search
for words to describe what's happening
right in front of them:
a woman punches a woman,
the hit strikes back,
and on it goes, and on,
until blood drips from cuts torn
and braided hair soaks sweat flowing.
And then, as if it were two men,
the commentators relax into it, talking
technique, tactics, until
some objection within
derails objectivity again,
and one of them says it, as if in pain:
not for me, women boxing.

It takes me back a decade or more
to an old boxer who swore:
the female body was not built to be hit.
And that was true, I remember thinking it,
before truth fogged over
like the eyes of a man hit
so hard his brain re-boots
as his boots wipe soles on air.

And a man's body was made for this?

Bedside Cabinet

Today the cabinet is full of clothes
lovingly washed, ironed, folded
as if on display in a shop,
photos arranged across the top,
toiletry bag packed with care.

Yesterday it was almost bare:
hospital soap, tissues, gown.
Now that patient's gone
home, to another ward, or
passed on, all trace

wiped out by a gloved hand;
what belongings there were
bagged; cabinet emptied.

Today the bed is surrounded
by concern and affection
materializing in attention
to detail; in every careful fold
of material.

Yesterday the only visitors
were busy strangers on duty –
waking, moving, washing,
feeding, injecting. Same
as today, minus the love

driven by helpless horror.
*What can we do but
be here for one another?*

The ABC 2

James came and turned
away from a right cross
in pain and walked across
    the street for a bottle.

Craig put on two stone of muscle,
boxed a man naturally heavier than him
and discovered the truth in
    there's nowhere lonelier than the ring.

Stewart had talent but lacked will,
won a few fights, missed nights
training, got a girl pregnant and
    no one knows where he went.

Graham went sixteen and two,
won a few district titles, a national,
boxed international and
    died inhaling aerosol.

Lesley was a Tomboy lesbo bitch
according to a few folk before
she learned to fight back and
    flattened Fat Mary on her back.

Alan wasn't very good – he got better,
lost a few before he won,
never won much but
    got there.

All six were in the same year.
James is on the dole now.
Craig is a bouncer.
No one knows where Stewart is.
Graham is in Kirk O' Beath Cemetery.
Lesley is at the university.

And Alan runs the local ABC
    three nights a week.

A Handshake in Thought

He almost broke my hand.
Ah'm a heavyweight, he explained
when I acknowledged his grip,
thinking, a heavyweight drinker,
as he stumbled into the bar snug
where I sat alone with a book and a beer.
We talked boxing.

He was a former champion.
Ah used tae spar wi Henry Cooper.
A gentleman, though best ye duck
Enry's Ammer.
His face looked as if ducking
had never been on his agenda.
A large fist caressed a dram.

Yi'r no fae roond here.
What ye in toun fir?
The poetry festival.
His features twisted.
Poetry n art say fuck all
tae fowk noo.
I handed him a poem.

I like to think he still has it
as I recall the way his eyes lit
as the world inside my words
gulped down deep inside of him
like a dram, leaving a warm
glow of recognition.
A connection was made,

like the handshake of two men,
unknown to each other,
reaching across a bar.

Chuvalo

No man knocked Chuvalo down.
After fifteen rounds with Ali,
Ali went to hospital;
Chuvalo went dancing with his wife.

Frazier hit him like a Pontiac at 100mph.
Foreman's fist was a big Mack truck
crashing into his face at 50mph.
Chuvalo's bone structure absorbed it all

like a tower shaken to its foundations
by the tremor of an earthquake.
Out on his feet, he would wake
and go on.

It was his sons that took him down.
One, two, three, gone to addiction;
with his wife the count reached four.
In the middle of his life

Chuvalo was lost in a dark room, alone.
An old man, he toured schools,
talking in a voice remarkably clear
after all the blows endured in a long career.

Footage shows him rocking back and forth.
Tears glisten in grooves that fists and time
scored upon his skin.
Teenagers listen,

rapt by and wrapped up in
a tone warm and deep as a cradling arm.
Chuvalo, strongest, toughest of men,
gathered all that was torn inside him

and reached out to them.
Love yourselves.
Love yourselves.
Love yourselves.

Adam's Terrace

for Stuart Wilson

'The past, he thought, is connected with the present in an unbroken chain of events flowing one out of the other. And it seemed to him that he had just seen both ends of that chain: he touched one end, and the other moved.'
Anton Chekhov, *The Student*

We'd crouch under fence-wire
and wander into a field.
Four brothers –
two wee boys, two auld men.
Easter tradition had us come
to roll our painted hard-boiled eggs
down a bank towards a burn,
re-enacting the resurrection;
boulder-eggs rolling, then
rising with us, climbing
like Sisyphus, whose myth
perhaps came closer
to the reality of men
who worked lives out
on earth and under it,
mining,
far from Eden.

Years later I'd learn
this was where they'd grown.
Foundations of their first home
still stub the earth like severed roots.
Adam's Terrace took its name
from the famous architect
whose estate remains nearby,
and whose buildings still stand,
masterpieces, dispersed
around the world.
The Terrace was built quickly
by the Fife Coal Company
who owned it.
They thought it dispensable.

When I recall us running
through a farmer's field,
I think not of miners' rows
or Adam's Eden, or Robert Adam
and the Enlightenment,
but the time that went
through my body like a voice,
one end of a line to another,
the connection a-waver,
never entirely clear, but there,
in me, like distant chatter
I can barely hear.

Should I close my eyes
and fall back on those fence-wires,
like a boxer stunned into the ropes,
I'd feel the lines take my weight
even as they stretch out of reach,
beyond vision, and imagine
the photo I have of those auld men
long since developed in my brain,
as wee boys in this field when
those brick-stub severed roots
budded walls, bloomed roofs,
and a stair exploded faces like a star
shooting one moment so far
into the lens the image blasted
decades deep into minds

like another picture never captured
by machine, but in me like a dream –
two wee lassies, sisters,
crouch under those fence-wires,
while the same wee boys
grown into men, fall back
as they look forward,
the past rising within them,
so strong they can taste
another time,
unique on each tongue,
like distinctly painted worlds,
released from hands
to find their own direction
over the same auld earth.

Flight

'It seems to me, O King, that the life of man on earth is like the swift flight of a single sparrow through the banqueting hall where you are sitting at dinner on a winter's day with your captains and counsellors. In the midst there is a comforting fire to warm the hall. Outside, the storms of winter rain and snow are raging. This sparrow flies swiftly in through one window of the hall and out through another. When he is inside, the bird is safe from the winter storms, but after a few moments of comfort, he vanishes from sight into the wintry world from which he came. So man appears on earth for a little while – but of what went before this life, or what follows, we know nothing.'
The Venerable Bede

It could be a hall, this 737,
though the people in it face forwards,
not towards each other, and the banquet
tastes like the plastic tray
it was served in.
We are travelling through the darkness,
500 mph, 35,000 feet,
my palm over your hand like a blanket.

A year before we met, Eve, my niece,
sat near me on a plane, shouting *hold on!*
because her Dey told her to –
her hand gripping the armrest;
her wee sister, girning behind me.

We took off seven years after
I'd shared a flight with my own Dey.
Then, I'd observed how his eighty-year-old face,
alive as the yet-to-be-born Eve's,
absorbed the new with the hunger of bairns
yet to arrive from nothing
and sit with him in the turn
of a few seasons.

In a few hours we'll land somewhere.
In a few hours we'll leave where we are.
Until then, let my hand cover your hand.
Until then, let us share
this brief flight together.

Notes

Thinking
Life is a nightclub across the road from Dunfermline Abbey, where King Robert the Bruce (1274-1329) is interred. Medieval makar Robert Henryson is thought to have lived in the Abbey area. No one knows when Henryson was born but he is thought to have died around 1508.

Ex-Factory Toun
The Cambridge University lecture on Adam Smith (1723-1790) was by Alan Macfarlane.

Ex-Mining Village, Xmas Day
'[T]here are still significant problems for the majority of Britain's coalfield communities such as; fewer jobs; lower business formation rates; higher unemployment rates; more people with serious health issues; higher numbers in receipt of welfare benefits and a struggling voluntary and community sector than national averages' (*The Coalfield Regeneration Trust*).

Antonine Wall, Croy Hill
The Antonine Wall (AD 142) was the northernmost frontier of the Roman Empire. It stretched between the Firth of Forth and the Firth of Clyde. The Glasgow Effect refers to the low life expectancy and poor health of residents in Glasgow, compared to residents elsewhere in Britain and Europe.

Daylight Robbery
Window tax: between 1696 and 1851 every household was taxed on the number of windows they had. The tax was hated because it was considered to be a tax on light and air. On April Fools' Day, 2013, the Bedroom Tax (Spare Room Subsidy) was enforced as part of the Welfare Reform Act of 2012.

Sticks 'n' Stones
Thomas Aikenhead (1676-1697), a student from Edinburgh, was the last person in Great Britain to be executed for blasphemy.

A Pint in Plato's Cave
The Fife mining village, Lumphinnans, was called Little Moscow when the Fife coalfields were a hotbed for communism.

The In-gaun Ee
Mine openings were known by Scottish coal miners as 'in-gaun een' – in-going eyes.

A Handshake in Thought
'A handshake in thought' was how Vincent Van Gogh signed off his letters. Enry's Ammer (Henry's Hammer) was the name given to British and European heavyweight champion Henry Cooper's left hook.

Adam's Terrace
The architect, William Adam (1689-1748) built Blairadam House in 1736. The estate was inherited by his son, the great architect, Robert Adam (1728-1792) in 1748. I grew up in the nearby village of Kelty, across the county borderline, in Fife. Growing up we referred to Blairadam House as 'the big hoose.' My Dey, Andrew Paterson, grew up in Adam's Terrace, Kelty, in the 1920s. The following evidence was presented to the Royal Commission on 13 October 1913, by Michael Lee. 'There are about 80 houses in Adam's Terrace very badly damaged by underground workings. In my opinion they are dangerous to life... All these houses belong to the Fife Coal Company, Limited. A number of the tenants have had to leave the houses owing to their unsafe condition.'

Glossary

Chakit: rough or unkempt. Crabbit: ill-tempered, in a bad mood. Dey: Grandfather in Fife. Girning: crying, weeping. Guddle: fish with the hands by groping under the stones or banks of a burn. Haar: cold sea fog on the east coast. Raws: miners' rows.

Acknowledgements

Thanks to the editors of the following publications in which some of these poems first appeared:

Ian Moir (ed) *Almost an Island: A New Anthology of Fife Writings* (2009), Kate Ailes (ed) *Aiblins: New Scottish Political Poetry* (2016) and WN Herbert and Andy Jackson (ed) *New Boots & Pantisocracies; Agenda (Broadsheet), The Crazy Oik, Drey, The Edinburgh Review, English Chicago Review, Fras, Glasgow Review of Books, Gutter, The Honest Ulsterman, Horizon Review, Ink Sweat & Tears, The Interpreter's House, The Literateur, the Morning Star, New Linear Perspectives, Northwords Now, The One O'Clock Gun, The Penniless Press, Poetry Salzburg Review, Poetry Scotland, The Poets' Republic, Prole, RAUM, Southlight* and *Wee Fictions*.

Some of these poems first appeared in the Calder Wood Press pamphlet, *The Heavy Bag* (2011) and in two *Poetry-For-All sma buiks* pamphlets (San Diego, California). Thanks to Robert Hansen.

Anithir Season was the subject of a filmpoem by artist Alastair Cook (2015).

Thanks to poets Christie Williamson and William Hershaw for their comments and suggestions on an early version of the manuscript, and to Magi Gibson and Gregor Addison at a later stage. Thanks to artist Ian Moir for all his help and support and for providing the artwork on the cover. Thanks to Gerry Cambridge and Gerry Loose. I gratefully acknowledge the support of the Clydebuilt apprenticeship scheme.

A special thanks to Lillian King for all her time and advice over the years.